Geri Schneider Winters

Kindle Best-selling author "Why Agile is Failing at Large
Companies (and what you can do so it won't fail at yours)"

I0041935

Do We Need
Managers?

Investigating Management's Role
in the Information Age

Ty yn Goch
Forrest
Publications
Albion, California

Published by Ty yn Goch Forrest Publications in 2018
First edition; First printing

Design and writing ©2018 Geri Schneider Winters
Cover design by Geri Schneider Winters
Author cover photo by Landers Photography, San Antonio, Texas

Any suggestions in this book are based on the author's own experience. They may or may not be relevant to your particular situation. The author and publisher do not guarantee any results you may achieve by following the suggestions in this book. Unless a specific company is identified, examples and stories are composites of several similar events and do not describe a specific person or company.

ISBN: 978-0-9967426-8-9

For additional book resources or to contact the author go to
www.geriwinters.com

As Always

For Jason

This book is for managers who want to be real contributors to their organization and for executives who are being pressed to make changes but do not know quite what to change or how.

Contents

Acknowledgements 9

Is There a Need for Managers? 11

What do Managers Do? 15

Envisioning the Company Direction 16

Communicating with Shareholders, Community, and Employees 17

Making sure there are Skilled People to do the Work 18

Making Sure the Right Work is Done 19

Reporting 19

Maintaining the Assets 20

The Rise of the Manager 23

Manufacturing 23

Transcontinental Railroad 25

World War II Impact on Management 26

Knowledge Age 27

Middle Management Anti-Patterns 31

Playing for Power 31

Very Lengthy Decision Making 32

Micro-managing 34

Endless Demands for More Reports 35

Privilege 36

Management in the Information Age 39

Without Managers, Who Does Management Work? 40

Setting Direction 41

People Management 42

Work Management 43

Reporting 45

Alternative Management Examples 49

Google Experiments 49

Google 2001 - No Line Managers 49

Google 2008 - What Makes a Good Manager 50

Menlo Innovations - No Middle Managers 52

The Morning Star Company - No Managers 53

Too Many Managers 57

How Many Directs Should a Manager Have? 57

How to Destroy a Startup 59

Reducing the Number of Managers 63

Remove a Layer of Middle Managers 64

Reduce the Size of a Management Layer.................. 66

Making Managers a Great Asset to the Company...........69

Resources 73

Google 73

Menlo Innovations... 73

The Morning Star Company...................................... 74

U.S. Industrial Revolution 74

Transcontinental Railway... 74

History of Management.. 74

Acknowledgements

Many thanks to my reviewers: Leigh (Bella) St. John, Thomas Meloche, and Carson Holmes. The book is much better due to their recommendations. Any remaining errors are my fault, not theirs!

While I will not name people or companies, my thanks go out to all the bad examples I have seen in my long career. These bad examples of company structure and management styles inspired me to write this book. I hope this book will motivate conversation and change to the betterment of all.

Is There a Need for Managers?

In November 2017 I attended AgileCamp Silicon Valley. One of the keynote speakers, Doug Kirkpatrick, told an amazing story of a company without managers, The Morning Star Company. I am aware of a number of mostly small, relatively new companies that are experimenting with getting rid of managers (or not having any from the start). Some are successful, some are not. What intrigued me about The Morning Star Company is that it is not a new company and it is not a small company. It is not an information company either. They are the world's largest producer of tomato paste for the packaged food industry. This is a company over 20 years old with about 400 full-time employees, nearly 2000 additional employees when tomatoes are processed, and no managers.

I have had a feeling for a long time that the many layers of middle managers I see at companies of all sizes are extraneous. I have seen small startups add layer after layer of managers as they grow. I remember one startup in the dot com boom that had more managers than engineers. Often those managers seemed to have very little to do. It seemed to me that a deep hierarchy existed largely because no one knew how else to operate, not because all those managers were needed.

I decided to challenge the assumption that it is necessary to create a hierarchy to run a company. In this book, I investigate the work managers do and consider how much of it has to be done by a manager. I consider the evolution of management, the problems that arise when too many managers have too little to do, and the factors that are driving the manager role to change. I end with some examples of different models that have been tried and draw some conclusions about how companies that wish to be leaner and more efficient can change their structure and management roles.

What do Managers Do?

Before addressing the need for managers, it is important to know what managers do. When running a company of any kind there are tasks that need to be done for the company itself. These tasks are independent of creating a product, selling a product, or marketing a product. These include things such as:

- envisioning the company direction
- communicating with shareholders, community, and employees
- making sure there are people with the right skills to do the work
- making sure the right work gets done in the right time for the right price
- reporting to shareholders, employees, government, and regulatory agencies
- maintaining the company infrastructure and assets, physical and virtual

No matter the structure of the company, these tasks have to be done by someone. Traditionally, these kinds of tasks are the responsibility of some kind of manager.

Many company owners like to have one person to hold accountable and responsible for these tasks. In a very small company, there is no need to designate managers to do the work because ownership of a task is clear. In larger companies, where these kinds of tasks may be distributed over a large number of people, having a manager in charge makes it clear who is responsible. Without a manager, there is the fear that if everyone is responsible then no one does the work.

Envisioning the Company Direction

The Board of Directors (BOD) represents the interests of the owners of the company. In some closely held companies, the BOD may be the owners of the company. In other companies, there are many shareholders, too many for a BOD. These shareholders are represented by people that the shareholders elect to serve on the BOD.

The BOD is responsible for setting the long-term direction of the company. This is almost always done in consultation with the executive leadership of the company. Executive leadership includes people such as CEO (Chief Executive Officer) responsible for the company products and services, CIO (Chief Information Officer) responsible for company data and information needs, CFO (Chief Financial Officer) responsible for company finances, COO (Chief Operations Officer) responsible for keeping the company running, and possibly others.

The long-term direction of the company includes the company vision. What is this company about? What do we do? What is important to us? How do we express that vision over the next 5 years or 10 years? The BOD looks at the current markets, but also looks at trends and tries to anticipate their impact on the company.

Executive leadership is responsible for setting yearly goals that are aligned with the company vision and move the company in the long-term direction set by the BOD. In some companies, executives are intimately familiar with the work of the company. In other cases, executives know very little about the company they lead. Executive leadership may reach out to other people in the company to get their input as to what is feasible. Ideally, these are people who are involved in the day-to-day work of the company. In a hierarchical company, the executives are most likely to ask some level of manager for their input.

Communicating with Shareholders, Community, and Employees

Executive leadership is responsible for communicating progress toward company goals to the BOD and shareholders. They often do not have complete information, and so they depend on getting information from people involved in the day-to-day work of the company. In a flat company, the information comes directly from the people doing the work. In a hierarchical company, the executives depend on some level of manager to provide this information.

Executives are also responsible for making sure everyone working for the company understands the company vision, long-term direction, and the goals for the year. Not only should the information be shared, but there needs to be opportunity for people doing the work to ask clarifying questions. In a small company executives can interact directly with the line workers. In larger companies, executives depend on managers to communicate the goals and answer questions.

A company is part of multiple communities. There will be one or more communities where employees live and work that are impacted by the company's presence. A company will typically be part of some industry with other similar companies and a company often depends on partners to accomplish its purpose. Executives also belong to communities of their peers. It is important for executive leadership to form and maintain relationships with the local communities, industry groups, partners, and peers in order to identify and resolve issues, detect trends or legal changes, and ensure the smooth flow of products and services. Executives often depend on some level of manager to help do this work.

Making sure there are Skilled People to do the Work

People management tasks are commonly done by managers. It is not usual for a stranger to walk in the door of your company, sit down at a desk, add themselves to payroll, and start working. (While open-source development is very close to this model, companies do not generally work this way.)

Managers detect the need for additional staff, locate people suitable for the job, and make sure there is a way to pay them for their work. If there is a problem with someone working at your company, a manager detects that there is a problem and works with the other person to resolve it. The resolution may mean the other person no longer works for your company, and a manager has to be responsible for removing them from places such as payroll, benefits, and access to systems.

In today's fast changing world, pretty much every person working should expect to need to learn more things throughout their career. A few examples of things to learn could include: how to use new equipment, how to use new software, more information about an industry, more information about laws that impact a job, how to lead others, or how to do a new process. Managers make sure that every employee has the information they need to do their current job or to change to a new job by providing documents, training, mentoring, or coaching.

Sometimes people do not get along. Often they can resolve the issue between themselves. But sometimes they do not. For the good of the company and the people involved, a manager detects these kinds of situations and helps get them resolved. This may involve coaching the people involved or leading mediation between the parties. The manager is also expected to know when it is appropriate to get Human Resources or Legal involved in resolving the issue.

Making Sure the Right Work is Done

Work management tasks are commonly done by managers. Executives and the Board of Directors set the company direction and goals for the company as a whole. Any work done in the company should be in support and fulfillment of the direction and goals. Work also needs to be prioritized to be sure the most important work is completed. Typically managers ensure that the work being done is in line with corporate direction and the highest priority work is completed in a timely manner.

How much it costs to run a company, develop products, or provide services is important information for the executives and Board of Directors. The information is needed for decisions concerning corporate direction and goals and has to be reported to agencies such as the IRS. In a very small company where everyone reports directly to executive leadership, the executives collect this information and do the reporting personally. In most companies, collecting this information and creating the reports is the responsibility of managers.

Closely related to budget, the executives and Board of Directors need to know when some work will be completed. They may need to ensure that regulatory or legal requirements are met by a certain date, or need to coordinate a release with a partner or vendor. In a very small company, executives collect the information and do the reporting, but in most companies managers do this work.

Reporting

Companies are required by law and regulation to produce many different kinds of reports. When executives are not closely in touch with the work of the company, reports are also needed to communicate consolidated information from line workers to executives. Ensuring income and expenses are properly categorized, managing data, collecting data, and preparing reports are tasks that have become a major responsibility of managers.

Some kinds of reports that managers create include quarterly and yearly financial reports to the Board of Directors and shareholders, tax returns to the IRS and state governments (monthly and yearly), compliance reports to regulatory agencies, reports on the market and competitors, reports on customers and their expectations, expense reports, progress reports, and efficiency reports.

The data for these reports has to be kept up-to-date at all times. Managers may do that work themselves or ensure that the people working for them are keeping the data up-to-date. Ultimately, the manager is responsible for the currency of the data, collecting the data, and generating the reports correctly and on time.

Maintaining the Assets

A company with a physical location needs to buy or rent buildings, furnish the buildings, provide equipment needed to do the work of the company, be sure the buildings are kept clean and maintained, be sure supplies are kept on hand, and usually have some way to limit access to the physical plant. Even virtual companies generally have some physical presence, possibly in the form of computers provided every employee. Except in the smallest of companies, executives depend on managers to make sure all those things happen.

Similar to the physical assets, most companies will have virtual assets. There are domains to acquire, websites to maintain, cloud-based applications to license, software applications to purchase, virtual meeting spaces to obtain, remote access to physical systems provided, and security has to be considered for all these needs. Except in the smallest of companies, executives depend on managers to make sure all those things happen.

The Rise of the Manager

In a small company, executive leadership, typically the founder or owner, can do all the tasks that are needed to run the company. Think about small businesses in your community, such as a dry-clean laundry, family-owned restaurant, or car wash. The owners are typically there every day, working side-by-side with their employees, doing whatever needs to be done to run the business. "Executive leadership" is often one or two people, the owners of the company. There are either no other managers or only line managers. (Line managers are people directly managing the people doing the work.) The role of middle manager came with the growth of large companies.

Manufacturing

Early to mid-1800 saw the rise of manufacturing in the United States. Prior to this time, businesses were generally small, local concerns. As companies grew larger, it was no longer possible for the owner or CEO to do all the work that was needed to run the company.

Before 1800, most people owned their own business or worked directly for someone who owned their own business. Businesses were things such as farm, pub, inn, general store, blacksmith, cobbler, weaver, tailor, yarn spinner, dye maker, doctor, veterinarian, wood worker, or stone worker. A common business pattern was the owner was the master craftsman doing the work requiring great skill. The owner in turn directed the work of journeymen and apprentices who performed the tasks requiring less skill. There was also a lot of cottage industry, where work such as spinning, weaving, and dying was done in people's homes. There were some large enterprises, primarily churches and the military, but most people were employed in small businesses.

Even government was small. In the early days of the United States, government was localized, focused mostly in cities. State governments were small with less power than the cities, and the federal government was quite small and the least powerful of all. (For a fascinating picture of the United States in the early 19th century read "Democracy in America" by Alexis de Tocqueville, published as volume 1 in 1835 and volume 2 in 1840. You can find these volumes on Project Gutenberg.)

When all the businesses are small and local, there is not much need for management. The master/owner directs the work of the employees as needed. More skilled employees are expected to do their work with little or no direction and to guide the work of less skilled employees.

Manufacturing changed all of this. Craftsman and cottage industries were replaced by factories full of machines. This required people who could tend the machines, but who did not need the skills to do work such as weaving, making shoes, or making furniture. Unlike crafts and cottage industries that required skilled labor, the factories could run on relatively unskilled labor. But because the labor force was unskilled, they required more oversight and direction of their work. And because there were so many people working at a factory, the owner could no longer oversee everyone. The role of manager was developed in order to direct the work of large numbers of people.

In the early part of the 19th century, managers were almost exclusively line managers, that is they managed the assembly lines. The focus of management was on efficiency; managers looked for ways to make each task of an assembly line faster and cheaper. Just as scientists observed and measured scientific processes, managers observed and measured the assembly line for the purpose of improving it. Managerial roles directly correlated with segments of a manufacturing process or an assembly line, so an organizational chart looked like a chart of the process or assembly line.

As a side note, this is where the terms line worker and line manager came from. The line worker worked on the assembly line. The line manager managed some part of the assembly line and the people working on that section of the assembly line.

Transcontinental Railroad

In 1862, the United States government passed a bill to fund the building of a transcontinental railroad. This was the largest project ever attempted at that time. The project was awarded to the Central Pacific and the Union Pacific Railroad companies, one working east to west the other working west to east to complete the railroad.

Many different kinds of managers were required to keep the project on time. Managers were responsible for: supply chain, logistics (especially of long jobs such as bridge and tunnel building), directing surveys and engineering, general supervisor of crew bosses, and financials. There was also a need for coordination with the US Government, US Army, and between the Central Pacific and Union Pacific railroad companies. All of this could not be done by executive management of the two railroad companies. The project required the use of managers to organize and oversee all the different parts of the project over long distances and many years.

Many people working on the transcontinental railroad were retired from the Civil War armies. From their Army days they had experience building railroads and doing other large projects.

They were also accustomed to working in a hierarchy of command. Executives from the railway companies looked to the Army for an example of how to organize the workforce using middle management layers.

It was necessary to add hierarchies of managers due to the sheer number of people involved and the distance between them. The actual numbers are not known, but at any given point in time, it is estimated there were 25-30,000 people working in some capacity on the railroad. While line managers made sure the work was getting done, middle managers made sure that the work was ordered in the most efficient way, that supplies got to where they were needed on time, that surveys were completed in time for engineering to be completed so that workers were not delayed in laying track, and that reports were made to the U.S. government so that everyone could be paid for their work.

The success of the transcontinental railroad was widely studied in the United States and abroad, and the effectiveness of an organization structured like the military with processes like an assembly line was widely acknowledged.

World War II Impact on Management

Post world war two saw a great increase in civilian industry. Veterans entered management schools in large numbers. Business schools were reinventing the role of managers to be more about logistics of people, supplies, facilities, and production since this was a key aspect to winning the war. Managerial positions became less about managing a process and making it more efficient, and more about delivering commands from superiors to subordinates. Management in general saw business as a machine and focused on logistics to run the machine, using command and control as the fundamental way business was run.

Managerial roles directly correlated to positions of power,

so an organization chart looked like a military hierarchy, with little relationship to the company business. In the United States, the belief grew that managers did not need to know how to do the work, they just needed to know how to manage the workers. Managers were increasingly removed from the day-to-day business of the company.

Knowledge Age

One historical justification for a middle manager role was to pass information from executives about the work to be done to the people doing the work. Middle managers also passed status of the work from the workers to the executives.

As information has become more and more automated, executives can easily share information directly with everyone employed in the company, without needing middle managers to carry the message. In turn, work management tools can instantly and in real time provide status to anyone who wishes it. Today it is easy to coordinate work over large distances without needing layers of middle managers to pass information from location to location.

At the same time that automation has mostly removed the need for people to pass information between executives and workers, the need to manage workers is also greatly reduced. A very large percentage of work today is knowledge work not physical labor. The work force is educated and self-motivated with tools that let them collaborate as needed with people anywhere in the world. Line workers are professionals who typically know more about their work than their boss does. They do not need to be told what to do or even how to do it.

With increased automation of information and collaboration,

along with an educated motivated workforce, today's companies need far fewer managers than in the past. In most modern companies, leadership is much more necessary than management. Only a few leaders are needed to provide direction to large numbers of people. Yet executive leadership in many companies are stuck in a traditional mindset that leads them to believe they require a large management team.

Middle Management Anti-Patterns

Companies of all sizes structure their management teams into layers. The line mangers are directly involved in the day-to-day business of the company. Between the line managers and executives are typically other managers to coordinate and communicate between executives and line managers. These are the middle managers of a company.

Middle managers are in a position to provide clear direction. Because they are not involved in the day-to-day running of the organization, they can take a big picture view of their organization. They can look for inefficiencies and find more efficient ways to get the job done. Or they might find teams that are extra productive and share their better way of working with other teams. A good middle manager is a true asset to their company.

Unfortunately too many middle managers are not very involved in running their organizations and instead spend their time maneuvering for personal gain. These middle managers are harmful to the company, each one causing waste up to millions of dollars a year. You can identify these toxic middle managers by the anti-patterns they display.

Playing for Power

In far too many companies I see middle managers spend their days in power plays. Meeting after meeting is focused on coming up with justifications for increasing their responsibilities and adding people to their chain of command. They may be asking for new responsibilities or trying to "steal" responsibilities from another middle manager. These meetings are intended to create a proposal for restructuring that will be presented to managers higher in the company at another meeting. Since other managers do not want this one to get more power, they will also be at those meetings presenting counter proposals. All of which have to be studied and analyzed and discussed endlessly.

Though the justification of all of this will be to make the company faster, better, cheaper, etc., most of these efforts do nothing at all for the company (except waste money). The purpose of these power games is for a middle manager to get promoted. Then he or she will continue to play power games at the next higher level of management.

If the managers were actually responding to the needs of their employees and the company while playing power games, it would not be quite so bad. But typically the middle managers are so busy playing power games that they do not have time to do real work such as providing input to a critical question that is blocking a project from completing. They are so focused on manuvering for postion, they do not have working relationships with other middle managers to resolve interdepartmental issues. These managers have replaced valuable work with power games.

Endless power games are a sign that the company has far too many middle managers.

Very Lengthy Decision Making

In command and control type organizations, there is no room for failure. Every manager from the top of the company down to project and line managers always has to be right. They have to propose the right budget, the right product, or the right guess on a competitors move. Every decision to be made has to be right.

In this kind of organization, a lot of time and effort is put into research and analyzing before a decision is made. Decisions take a really long time to make because they have to be right. Positioning is determined so that if it turns out the manager is not right, there is someone or something else to blame. That someone or something else to blame will be outside of the manager's control.

The more layers of management there are, the worse the problem gets, because each manager at every level is trying to avoid making a decision. They are spending a lot of time figuring out their position if they have to make a decision, especially what they will do if something goes wrong. In a flat company, where there are fewer people that have to make a decision, having to always be right does have some impact on the company. But the more managers that have to be right in the chain of decision making, the longer it takes to make a decision.

Other companies have very lengthy decision making because they claim to be highly collaborative. Every decision has to involve anyone who could be impacted so that each person has the opportunity to express their thoughts. There are many, lengthy meetings to talk things over until everyone is in agreement on the action to take. The more people involved, the longer the collaborative decision making takes to complete.

In some cases, the managers never make the decision, and eventually someone who needed the answer makes a choice because they have no more time to wait. I have seen this happen fairly frequently in project based companies. The project is coming to an end, the product is being delivered, and the team cannot wait any longer for an answer. So the delivery team makes the decision. Many teams in this position will say "It is easier to ask forgiveness than permission". Unfortunately this often means that someone who does not know all the consequences is making the decision on behalf of the company.

Very lengthy decision cycles make a company less effective and efficient. When I say very lengthy, I mean times that are far longer than a reasonable person would expect. I have seen a simple question with well documented answers, with the benefits and potential downsides clearly specified for each choice, spend over 6 months in management meetings being discussed over and over. No one wanted to make even a simple decision with clear consequences. I have seen complicated questions take a year or more.

Very lengthy decision cycles are a sign of having too many middle managers, too many people involved in the decision making process.

Micro-managing

In some companies, I have seen middle managers at the level of vice president reviewing small, minimal impact decisions made by project managers many levels below them. Vice presidents should not need to sign off on $1000 budget item. Directors should not need to review a training presentation to approve the wording, especially when it is a topic they know nothing about. When middle managers are that involved in the day-to-day running of the company, they are micro-managing.

In some cases, the middle managers do not trust the employees to do the job correctly. They usually do not understand the work, but they still feel they must oversee it. This is time consuming and frustrating for the people doing the work. Typically a line worker has to go to a meeting with the middle manager to explain something they have produced line by line or slide by slide. Then they listen to the feedback offered on how the slide could be better worded, or why the manager does not like a particular image, or even how the code could be improved. Then usually there is a conversation about how the wording cannot be changed because it will change the meaning, or the image is an industry standard logo, or the code has to be the way it is in order to work. I once heard a middle manager ask if the code could be refactored to be smaller so it would weigh less, a statement that made no sense and was of no use to anyone. This kind of micro-managing activity can go on for weeks and provides no value.

Some middle managers micro-manage because it makes them feel important. Many middle managers do not really have much to do. They have too much time on their hands. They are afraid of being found redundant. So they create work that makes them appear important to the company. Many business processes include a series of sign-offs that are justified as being needed for risk or compliance reasons. Many of those sign-offs are actually not needed for risk or compliance, but they are needed to show that a middle manager has an important job.

Middle managers getting involved in the details of their employees' work is a sign that there are too many middle managers in the company.

Endless Demands for More Reports

In some companies, the number of reports generated is far larger than it needs to be. The reports are almost always overlapping, with a lot of redundant information. Line workers and their direct managers end up spending a lot of time creating these reports, even in companies where the same information can be easily found by looking online. Middle managers do not look online; they want someone else to create a nice paper report or presentation for them. After spending the time putting a report or presentation together, then the person who created it gets to spend time meeting with the middle manager to explain it.

Sometimes middle managers ask for their employees to spend a lot of time creating reports because the reports make the middle manager look important. They have collected a lot of information and spent a lot of time reviewing it with their employees. But this takes the line workers away from the work of the company. In today's world of automation of information, there is not much need for people to produce paper reports and presentations. Automated dashboards give the information in real time by anyone who cares to look.

I once knew of a fairly large project that had a team of twenty managers whose entire job was to produce paper reports for the various middle managers and executives concerned about the project. All of this information already existed in an online executive dashboard that was updated in real time. A vice president of the company convinced executive leadership that all those people and paper reports were necessary to the project. I was not impressed with the reports, but I was impressed with the vice president's ability to sell waste to the executives.

Asking for lots of reports and presentations can be a sign that there are too many middle managers in the company.

Privilege

In some companies, executives and middle managers are very conscious of their privileges. Anyone who is an executive has vice presidents working for them. They could not possibly work with directors or lower; that would be insulting the rank of the executive. Similarly, vice presidents have directors reporting to them.

This attitude leads to unnecessary layers of management, just for reasons of status. I have been in a large company that in between executive and line manager they had senior VP, VP, junior VP, senior director, director, and manager, for a total of 9 layers of management. Any particular project in that company had at least 4 people with manager in their title that the project team had to report to directly (not including the project manager). And each of those 4 managers had different directors above them, reporting to different VPs with different agendas. The project managers spent most of their time creating reports for all those managers and meeting with the managers to explain the reports.

This ranking system also comes about because of the idea that someone has to be continuously promoted to "higher ranking" positions in order to be seen as successful at the company. As a company grows larger, higher ranking positions are created just so someone can be promoted. I have been in companies that had directors with no one working for them. Someone needed to be promoted to a higher rank because of the results of their performance appraisal, so they got promoted to director with essentially nothing to do.

Some of the reasons that companies have a lot of layers of management is the outdated idea that a manager should only have around 10 directs (people working directly for them). While that may be true if you have to directly oversee someone's work, in today's companies few people need or want that high degree of management. With well-educated, self-managing people and automation of information, one person can be a manger of far more than 10 people.

If a large company has more than 3-4 levels of management above line worker, it almost certainly has too many middle managers. If a small company has more than 2 levels of management above line worker, it almost certainly has too many middle managers.

Management in the Information Age

Most companies today have a variety of initiatives in place to become more efficient in an effort to drive down costs and reduce time to market. Power based hierarchical management structures are not efficient by their very nature. These kinds of structures were initially adopted from military practice. But today's military units have changed from a top-down command and control structure to one that gives more authority to the person on the front line. Thins change occurred because the old structures were too inefficient. Modern companies would do well to consider ways to reduce management overhead and increase efficiency.

The nature of work has radically changed from more physical labor to an educated knowledge based workforce. Line workers today usually just need to know what needs to be done. They do not need to be directed how to do the work. Often the work can be described in relatively broad terms, with the educated, skilled employee making the best choices for how to do the work. Leaders, facilitators, coordinators, and coaches provide the support the line workers need to do their work most effectively.

Because information is readily available to anyone with a computer, there is little need for a group of managers to pass information back and forth between executives and workers. Long decision cycles involving many layers of management are typically quite unnecessary. More decisions can be trusted to people closer to the work and most decisions can be made by fewer people.

There is less and less work for large numbers of middle managers to do. Middle management anti-patterns may evolve because people have too little work to do and they are trying to look valuable.

Not only is this a bad thing for the managers (to feel they are not of value), but the anti-patterns have a toxic effect on the whole company. Having fewer managers means the remaining ones will have plenty of valuable work to keep them busy. This removes the time and motivation for the anti-patterns.

Without Managers, Who Does Management Work?

As discussed at the start, there is work that managers do that still has to be done. This includes setting direction, people management, work management, and reporting. This can all be done without managers as long as appropriate systems, processes, procedures, and contracts are in place. Those systems, processes, procedures, and contracts should exist anyway for the managers to follow, so this is not a large burden. A company may still wish to have specific people identified to do this work (whether or not they are called managers). Otherwise, the line workers will have less time to do their work in order to perform tasks that had previously been done by their manager.

For efficiency, a company will want to reduce the number of people in a chain of information. Instead of passing requests down an information chain and waiting for responses to come back up, those who want the information can go directly to the source of information without an intermediary. If an executive wants to know about how things work day-to-day, then ideally the executive should seek out senior staff members (not their managers) and ask about the work.

If a company does not wish to have managers, then this work has to be done either by the BOD, executive leadership, or line workers. Before getting rid of or reducing the number of managers in a company, executive leadership has to answer the question "who will do the work that the managers used to do". The work still has to be done and you cannot expect people to just pick it up and do it. Companies that fire all the managers without preparation find themselves with all kinds of problems.

Setting Direction

Wise leadership will get input from the line workers as part of their envisioning of the direction of the company and goals for the year. Traditionally managers have worked with executive leadership to set yearly goals. The down side to this approach is that today we have a class of professional managers who know very little about the work of the people they manage. In setting yearly goals, what the executives need are people who do the job to assess the feasibility of the proposed goals.

Without managers, the BOD and executive leadership will either interact directly with everyone (in a small company) or will interact with senior staff to get their input. In smaller companies, this could be done by involving everyone in an envisioning workshop. Surveys could be used to elicit ideas. In larger companies, where it is infeasible to get input from everyone (due to size), senior people from different areas can be included in goal setting. A senior accountant, senior customer support representative, senior salesperson, senior marketing person, enterprise architect, or senior business intelligence expert might be invited to meet with leadership to give input.

Once the yearly goals are set, they need to be communicated to everyone. In a small company, a town hall type meeting could be held with everyone gathered together. Plenty of time should be allowed for everyone to be sure they understand the goals for the year and how those goals apply to them personally. In larger companies, the senior staff who were involved in setting the goals would share the information with their more junior colleagues. If less experienced staff need help determining what work needs to be done to achieve the yearly goals, senior staff would guide that discussion.

People Management

It does not actually require a manager to hire people nor to let them go. People doing the work know if more people are needed. They also know who is not doing the job that needs to be done. Folks without human resources background might need to work with a colleague who does that kind of work in order to write a job description, review resumes, and fill out all the legal paperwork needed to hire someone. They might need to contact someone technical to set up accounts and get a computer on the person's desk.

Similarly with letting someone go, appropriate processes can be put in place that anyone can follow if they feel a person should no longer work for the company. A person who decides to let someone go can include colleagues in other areas to do the right legal paperwork and close accounts.

There are companies who have chosen for 20 years or more to let the line workers do the hiring and firing. With appropriate processes and guidelines in place, which you need with or without managers, there is no reason a team cannot hire and fire their own members. Even though it does take time out of the day-to-day work to go through a hiring process, many teams are happy to take the time because they prefer to have control over who they work with. When a team decides an individual does not fit, or an individual decides they do not fit the team, then the team should be able to let that person leave the team. This could be to a different team or it could mean the person leaves the company.

In general, people should be responsible for their own careers. Each individual should ensure they take the proper safety training every year, that they take classes to keep up with changes in their profession, or that they take continuing education credits to maintain certification. A "nag" application or team mates could help ensure individuals do not forget to complete any required training. Teams using Agile practices have regular retrospectives where they discuss how to continue to improve as a team. That kind of mechanism is a beautiful self-management technique for helping team members improve in their career without needing a manager's guidance.

With appropriate processes and guidelines in place, which you need with or without managers, there is no reason that an individual or team could not sign up for classes, find appropriate documents, or hire a coach. Where a manager could be useful is when multiple people or teams want the same training or coaching. Knowing this, a manager could schedule a large number of people for a class at the same time, or get one coach for multiple teams. But this could also be done using tools such as a community bulletin board. Someone could express an interest, other people could say they want it too, and all the people who want a class or coach could work together to organize it.

Sometimes people do not get along. Often they can resolve the issue between themselves. But sometimes they do not. For the good of the company and the people involved, someone needs to detect these kinds of situations and help them get resolved. This could be a manager, but there could also be defined processes in place that lead eventually to a person with an arbitrator role who helps resolve the issue if the people concerned have been unable to work it out between them.

Work Management

Once the teams understand what the company wants to do, and the priorities that have been set by executive management, generally the teams doing the work can figure out how to do the work and the best order to do it in. In many companies, there will be at least one layer of people between executives and workers. This layer of people (who might be called managers, coordinators, facilitators, team leads, or product owners) can be very useful to keeping an eye on the big picture of company goals and making sure the teams do not lose sight of what work is the most important (something very easy to do when focused on the day-to-day work).

How much it costs to run a company, develop products, or provide services is important information for the executives and Board of Directors. The information is needed for decisions concerning corporate direction and goals. Closely related to budget, the executives and Board of Directors need some idea of when work will be completed. They may need to ensure that regulatory or legal requirements are met by a certain date, or need to coordinate a release with a partner or vendor.

With all the opportunity to automate information sharing, it is very easy to create dashboards to show the required information in real-time. Of course this requires that people doing the day-to-day work keep information about their work (such as what work is planned, how much has been completed, what is the progress toward a larger objective, how many hours they spent working on a particular job or project, what purchases were made, or how much was sold) up-to-date in the tool. This is something that many people forget to do regularly, so someone making sure it happens can be very useful, whether that person is a team lead, scrum master, manager, or coordinator. Or perhaps it is a software application that does not let someone log out for the day until they update their time and work.

The line workers will know if they need upgrades to equipment or software to do their jobs, or if they need something new. If the workers know the budget for such purchases, a team of people can work together to decide on the best way to spend the money. They may decide it is more important to the team to buy some new equipment than to upgrade software this year. Transparency of budget, and letting the people who do the work make decisions about how to spend the money, is very empowering for the team.

When it is "their" money to spend, and they know how much it is, they will be careful about how that money is spent.

Reporting

With appropriate systems in place, the information needed to generate reports of various kinds, including the quarterly and yearly financial reports to the Board of Directors and shareholders, tax returns to the IRS and state governments (monthly and yearly), compliance reports to regulatory agencies, reports on the market and competitors, reports on customers and their expectations, expense reports, progress reports, and efficiency reports, should always be up-to-date and available. At the push of a button, the appropriate report is generated.

One thing that can be an issue for some companies is that work can be categorized as either capital or expense, and the right category has to be chosen based on the kind of work being done. This should be set up in information systems so most people never have to worry about it. Any job code should include the information about whether the work is capital or expense. A large percentage of the people in the company always do the same kind of work, so there is no need for someone to prepare a report categorizing that work. For the relatively small number of people who do both kinds of work, there should be published guidance that tells these folks when to categorize their work one way or another. They will need to keep track of their time, which is a reasonable thing to require. Then the information should be readily available through the timekeeping or payroll system.

The data for reports has to be kept up-to-date at all times. The foundation of the data is the time and effort spent by line workers, purchases, and sales. There may be additional data such as customer satisfaction surveys (which can be automated) and market information that also needs to be kept up-to-date. Each person who does something to create that data is responsible for making sure that information is always up-to-date. Peer pressure from team mates or an application that reminds someone to enter the data (a "nag" app) can replace managers. Personal experience suggests this is one management responsibility that is often better handled by having a designated person (whatever their role) ensure the data is entered by their team mates.

Alternative Management Examples

I t can be instructive to see what is being done at other companies. We hear about some extreme management experiments, but a lot of what makes the news comes from relatively young and small companies. How have relatively long lived and/or larger companies managed to keep from adding a large number of managers?

Google Experiments

Google was founded in 1998 by Larry Page and Sergey Brin, a couple of engineers with a great idea. Like many engineers, they had a great distrust of management of any kind. But as the company grew larger, a management layer was gradually added between Larry and the engineers. Twice Google has closely examined the need for managers. The results provide a great picture of what an effective management structure can be and why it is useful.

Google 2001 - No Line Managers

In 2001, Larry Page decided to get rid of all engineering managers. At the time, there were approximately 130 engineers and about 6 line managers. Page hired a new VP of Engineering and decided all the engineers would report to that one person. His rationale was that non-engineers should not be supervising engineers. One day there were 6 managers in engineering, the next day they were gone.

The problems over the next couple of months make it sound

like there was not a transition plan in place. There were problems in engineering such as projects were not getting staff or multiple projects were doing the same work. Engineers felt they were not getting feedback on their work. They did not know if they doing a good job or not. These kinds of problems indicate that no one picked up the work the managers had been doing. The new VP, a middle manager, was not doing the line managers' work and most of the engineers were not doing it.

As you will see below, other companies have shown that managers are not necessarily required. But to accomplish that objective requires having appropriate processes in place and making sure the tasks that managers do are handled by someone. It also requires the right people. Not every person wants to work in a self-managed environment. While some thrive in that environment, others do not.

Page ended up bringing the managers back after a few months. The problem was not too many line managers. Six line managers for 130 engineers is not at all unreasonable. Replacing line managers with one person in a middle management position did not make sense, as Page was told at the time. It was not until 7 years later that the actual problem was addressed.

Google 2008 - What Makes a Good Manager

In 2008, amid complaints from engineers about their managers, the Google people operations team (Human Resources) decided to apply data analytics to discover if there was any value to managers. They set out to study the managers to find out what the good ones were doing that people liked and what the bad ones were doing that people did not like.

They discovered that good managers were of great benefit to Google. Good managers increased job satisfaction, retention, and employment within their groups. With so many people in the

United States hating their jobs, this is all good news. The Google people operations team identified 8 characteristics of a good manager. Today they train and coach managers at all levels of the organization on these 8 characteristics and use them to measure performance.

Not only are there 8 characteristics of a good manager, Google has them listed in order of importance. What is a little surprising, given Page's contention that engineers should only be managed by engineers, is that technical knowledge turned out to be the least most important characteristic. Here are the 8 in order:

- Is a good coach
- Empowers the team and does not micromanage
- Expresses interest/concern for team members' success and personal well-being
- Is productive and results-oriented
- Is a good communicator – listens and shares information
- Helps with career development
- Has a clear vision and strategy for the team
- Has key technical skills that help him or her advise the team

Today, Google is not anti-manager, Google is against bad managers.

In 2013 Google had about 37,000 employees of which 5,000 were managers, 1,000 directors, and 100 vice presidents. That would be 6100 managers. Very roughly, 15% of the company employees were in management, with 30,900 in non-management roles. On average that is 6 directs per manager, 5 managers per director, and 10 directors per vice president. That is a very small number of directs per manager, looking more like traditional command and control companies rather than a lean, modern corporation.

Based on the 2013 numbers, Google could be much leaner in management positions. They probably did not need 2 layers of middle management (vice president and director), unless they were in a fast growth stage, quickly adding more line workers to fill in below the management layers. Given that the second most important characteristic of a manager is "Empowers the team and does not micromanage", I would expect a manager to have around 30 directs (or possibly up to 50) instead of 6.

Menlo Innovations - No Middle Managers

Menlo Innovations was founded in 2001 by Richard Sheridan, James Goebel, Robert Simms, and Thomas Meloche with a goal of bringing joy to the world through software. The company creates custom software for their clients.

From the beginning, the culture has been highly collaborative. Nearly everyone works in pairs and pairs change weekly. In this collaborative culture, there are no managers making hiring or firing decisions. The people doing the work of the company interview candidates, decide who will be hired, who will be promoted, and who will be let go.

The CEO, Rich Sheridan, does not have a corner office. He spends the day wandering around the floor, interacting with whoever needs his time and attention. The other executive is a COO. A "floor manager" assigns pairs each week. Project managers work directly with the clients (who are project sponsors) helping them identify business goals and prioritize the upcoming work so their budget is spent wisely. The project managers interact with the team much like a Scrum Master, addressing issues and removing obstacles. Team members can work directly with the client as well. They do not have to go through the project manager to work with the client. All of the managers are line managers; there are no middle managers at Menlo Innovations.

The company varies in size depending on the contracted projects they are working on. Generally it varies between 50-70 people. The largest project team they have had was 25 people.

Their small teams are very effective and get more done than much larger teams at other companies, partly because they do not have a lot of layers of management to interact with, and largely due to their high degree of collaboration.

In a company with no middle managers, the question becomes can you scale this model into a larger organization? Rich Sheridan thinks it might be done by creating new "cells" in other places. Split the current organization in half, move half to a different location, and then hire new people in both locations, much like the model followed by W.L. Gore & Associates. The upper limit in any particular location is most likely below 150, Dunbar's number. Since Rich cannot be in two places at once, if each location needs its own executive on site, it would require more people at the top of the company.

The Morning Star Company - No Managers

The Morning Star Company was founded by Chris J. Rufer in 1970 as a trucking company to haul tomatoes to other carriers. In 1982 he founded his first tomato paste processing plant. In 2013, the company had about 400 full time employees. This number grows to more than 2400 in tomato season.

Rufer founded his business on two key principles:

- Individuals should not use force against other people or their property.
- Individuals should respect and uphold the commitments they have made to others.

Adhering closely to those principles led to a company where every person is completely self-managed, including their seasonal labor force. The traditional functions of a manager (planning, coordinating, controlling, staffing, and directing) are handled by all members of the organization. There are no managers because manager work is done by everyone as an intrinsic part of their jobs. Everyone is a manager. There is no formal hierarchy.

This approach works due to their extensive use of contracts. Each employee (colleague) defines their own job in a Personal Commercial Mission statement which describes the colleague's contribution to the success of the company. This contract, instead of a person, is their "boss". Each year, the colleague negotiates their commitments and responsibilities with other colleagues in Colleague Letters Of Understanding (CLOUs). How people work together to get the job done is negotiated by the people doing the work. Colleagues hold each other accountable for the CLOUs they have negotiated. Morning Star has replaced managers with measurable contracts.

There are no job hierarchies and no promotions. An employee-elected compensation committee sets pay levels after comparing a person's performance against their CLOUs. Each colleague has complete autonomy to do what it takes to fulfill their obligations to the company. If they need to buy equipment, they buy it and send the bill to accounting. If they need a person with a new skill set, they hire someone who has the skills they think the company needs. If they need training, they sign up for a class, bill it to the company, and attend the class. There are processes and procedures in place to help colleagues resolve personal differences between themselves.

While there is no formal hierarchy, there are natural dynamic hierarchies. When a group of colleagues need to work together to achieve a purpose, it sometimes happens that it would be useful for one or another to lead the "project". This occurs naturally based on who has the right knowledge and has nothing to do with seniority. For example, if a colleague wants to hire someone they will find another colleague who understands HR to lead and guide them in the activities that need to happen to make a hire.

Along with self-management, Morning Star practices transparency and honesty throughout the company, with their suppliers and partners, and with the local community. There are no information silos and it is assumed everyone has a need to know.

This kind of company is not for everyone. Not everyone wants to negotiate their job with peers every year. Not everyone wants to talk with someone who is not doing their job properly. Some people do want to be told what to do. Some people want a position of power. Morning Star estimates up to 50% of the experienced people they hire leave within two years because they cannot adapt to the new way of working.

Too Many Managers

What you have read so far may lead you to think I am against managers. I am not against having managers. I think there are many people who do not want to work in a completely self-managed company such as Morning Star. I think a good manager can keep a group of people working smoothly together and be a real asset to their company. I am against having too many managers. I am against the traditional manager role that is about having power over other people. I am especially against having many layers of middle managers between executive leadership and the people doing the work.

How Many Directs Should a Manager Have?

In traditional, hierarchical companies a manager typically has 10 or fewer people working directly for him or her. In a situation where the manager came from senior staff and is in a role of training inexperienced people to do the job, 10 is a reasonable number of people. Considering that today most managers are not from senior staff and most teams are composed of a mix of seniority, team members will train each other and do not need a manager to train them. The manager needs far less interaction with their direct reports than was needed in the past.

By letting your educated, skilled employees manage themselves and their work, and letting people closest to the problem make the decision, a company can do without a large number of managers at all levels. Wise use of automation makes data collection easy.

Any particular manager can have a far larger number of people whose work they facilitate than they could in the past. With more self-management and appropriate automation, it is not infeasible to have one manager over 30-50 people, depending on the kind of work their direct reports do.

The only time this number of employees is an issue is if your company still does those once a year performance review exercises. Many companies have gone to a different approach, having reviews much more often and including tools such as 360 degree reviews. If you have 50 people to review, and for whom you have to create performance plans for the coming year, it is a lot of work. This job can be made easier by making notes year round about each employee, what they are working on, new challenges they are taking up, and how well they are doing. You can create performance plans throughout the year as well. Doing a little bit all the time is much less painful than trying to squeeze all the work into a couple of weeks.

With automation enabling someone to lead larger numbers of people, a company might be structured like this: executive leadership, up to 20 middle managers, up to 1000 managers (who ideally were promoted from senior staff), and up to 50,000 line workers. Making those 1000 managers into middle managers and adding a layer of up to 50,000 managers under them would allow for up to 2,500,000 line workers. That is only 2 layers of middle managers and 4 layers of management (executive to line manager) in total for a very large company. This structure has just a bit over 2% management, which is extremely lean. 2% management might be too lean. For many companies, a goal of 5-7% of their people in management is far less than they have today. Companies do not need to have so many layers of managers. Companies do not need so many managers in each layer.

This kind of leaner structure is important to all corporations. There is a large cost savings to the company by not paying so many managers. There is also a large time savings to the company, allowing it to deliver faster and respond to change quickly when needed. With fewer managers, you can afford to only hire the best managers. Google's study, referenced in the examples section, showed that teams with the best managers greatly outperformed other teams. Team members were happier and less likely to leave the company. By having only excellent managers, your company saves a lot of money and time due to greater productivity.

This matter of too many managers is not just a problem of large companies. Many startups are too quick to add managers as they grow. This may be caused by investors requiring the additional management layers or the founder thinking the additional managers have to be added because that is how companies grow. In both cases, managers at various levels are added because that is the only model known to investors or founders.

How to Destroy a Startup

A small Silicon Valley startup is illustrative of how quickly a company can become overloaded with managers. This company was founded by a guy with a great idea for a hardware product. He was self-funded and worked out of his garage, gradually adding more people to the project to do the work he was less skilled at.

The team got all the safety approvals, showed the machine at trade shows, and got enough pre-sales to send the machine out for manufacturing. The founder, like many founders, kept full control of the company. He was the only shareholder and so he had no board of directors or investors to report to. Staff were added for sales and marketing, the company moved into an office, and the founder added a general manager to oversee operations, sales, and marketing. The founder continued to manage engineering and the general manager contracted for services such as accounting and legal.

At one point, there were about 50 people in the company and 2 managers, the founder and the general manager. Then this company was bought by a much larger company which decided to manage it as a wholly owned subsidiary. The founder and general manager were replaced with a CEO, 2 vice presidents, and 4 directors. None of these people were engineers. Since none of them understood engineering, 4 managers were hired to direct the work of the line workers. This is how the big company understood management.

Instead of 2 managers directing the line workers, there were now 4 managers and an additional 7 people who had nothing to do with the day-to-day work of the company. Instead of one person to report to and get direction from, line workers now had 4 layers of management giving direction, frequently contradicting each other, and rapidly changing priorities. Instead of talking to one person about the work and how it was going, line workers had to create reports about the work.

Since most of the managers did not understand the work of the company, they kept asking for more and more information in their effort to understand, especially on the engineering side. Productivity dropped dramatically and many of the most senior people left the company. The parent company decided to add more departments and more managers so they could hire more people to get productivity back up. To keep costs down, company management replaced senior people with new hires.

In a two year period, that former lean, productive, very successful company became one bogged down in bureaucracy and reports. Morale was poor, productivity was down, and the parent company was not seeing the return they expected on their investment. Their ideas for how to fix the problem were only making matters worse. They needed a CEO who understood a hardware product company and perhaps 4 managers from senior staff who reported to the CEO. There was no need for the vice presidents and directors. They were only hired because the parent company thought that was the way it was supposed to be.

Unfortunately, I have seen this pattern very often in Silicon Valley. Too many managers in a very small company has consistently led to failure.

Reducing the Number of Managers

For those companies that decide to reduce the number of managers, it is important to plan how this will be done. One bad approach is to fire some managers one day and hope people figure out how to make it work for themselves. Another bad approach to reducing the number of managers is to change manager titles so they no longer have the word manager in the title. (That was a real life strategy from a government contractor that was told they had too many managers – change the title but not the job).

Now is the time to train all managers at every level in leadership and coaching skills. If the managers continue to manage as they did in the past, but with a larger number of direct reports, they will be vastly overworked. If they are not good at it already, they need to learn to lead and guide and let their teams manage themselves.

If you are going to truly reduce the number of managers, there will be fewer people working for your company. People will either leave on their own or they will be let go. This is a hard thing to do for everyone concerned. How the change to the company is communicated can make matters worse or better. This is a good time to be especially careful to communicate well and often, and to make time for people to get their questions answered.

For many companies, the right approach is gradual change over time. Making big change is disruptive of business, relationships, and culture. Instead of looking to change the whole company at once, change could be made division by division or department by department. A very small company, such as my example 50 person

Silicon Valley company, will likely make the change all at once since there are so few people involved. A company that size is also likely to see dramatic immediate improvement.

Widespread short-term change is so hard that it is most commonly done when there is a big change in leadership at or near the top of the company. A board of directors will often hire a new CEO from outside the company with the purpose of making these kinds of changes. This is such a difficult job that this CEO may be called the "hatchet man" and generally this CEO is greatly disliked. Usually these CEOs do not stay long after the corporate restructuring. They get the job of restructuring the company done and then are replaced by someone else who rebuilds the company culture under the new company structure.

The other time that widespread short-term change occurs is when the company is in crises. If something radical is not done, the company will literally fail and everyone will be out of a job. Once the company recovers, it is especially important to not restore the management layers it had before. Often having too many managers in a medium or small sized company is one of the causes of the crises. In that situation, bringing back all the managers once the crises is over just brings the problem back again, this time to complete failure.

Remove a Layer of Middle Managers

Companies that want to reduce the number of layers of middle managers may want to remove one layer at a time to reduce disruption. If the company has executives, vice presidents, directors, managers, and line managers the first change might be to remove the layer of directors. This middle layer is the least connected to the company. Directors do not work directly with executives nor with line workers. It is more likely that their job is simply passing information back and forth.

Without directors, managers report directly to vice presidents. Each vice president will have more direct reports. This will require some adjustment to how the vice president is used to working. Training and coaching in how to handle more directs may be required in some cases. This may also require changes at the executive level when vice presidents have less time to devote to the executives' needs. Some vice presidents will not like the changes and will choose to retire or leave to work for another company.

What to do with the directors you no longer need? Some may choose to retire or leave to work for another company. Others may choose to take open manager positions. What happens to their pay in this case? Does it change or not? Those leading the transformation should take the opportunity to find toxic directors (see the anti-patterns section) and let them go. There may also be toxic vice presidents that you choose to let go and some directors may be moved into those positions. Directors moved into vice president roles will also need training and coaching to understand their new responsibilities. In the restructuring, you may have some vice presidents with too many direct reports and others with very few. There may be a need to move managers under a different vice president than they worked for previously.

This kind of transformation should be done over a relatively large period of time. A very large company might take a year or two to transform the entire corporation. A small or medium sized company might get it done in a month or two. That may sound like too much time, but you need to decide on an approach, have training and coaching resources in place, and create all the communication pieces you need to communicate the changes and the reasons for them. Especially in big companies, legal may need to be involved. Human resources will definitely be involved in all cases.

Reduce the Size of a Management Layer

Some companies may be relatively flat already and may just want to reduce the size of a layer of managers. Assume that there are two line managers and each one has 6 people reporting to them. If all 12 people report to one line manager (which should be an easy change) you remove the need for one of the managers. It is more common for line managers to have relatively large teams already, so most likely this kind of change will occur in the middle management layers.

This change is less disruptive than removing a whole layer of management. The hierarchy stays the same, each manager just has more people working for him or her. Planning is still very important. You probably only want to change one layer at a time, i.e. only reduce the number of directors but keep the number of vice presidents the same until the first change is complete.

You also want to think about how many direct reports make sense for each manager and decide how quickly you want to reach that number. In the example of Google, where the average number of direct reports was 6, if you have a goal of 20-25 direct reports per manager you could either merge 4 teams under one manager all at once, or you might do it in two stages. Going from 6 direct reports to 25 is challenging and yet very possible. Having tools and coaches in place to help a person manage the new larger team is a really good idea. If you have a goal of 50 direct reports per manager, going from 6 to 50 is a radical change requiring a lot of coaching support for the managers with suddenly very large teams. That kind of change is probably better in two or more stages.

When thinking about the number of direct reports for a manager, think about what else that manager needs to do. Vice presidents typically spend a lot of time with executive leadership, supporting them in their jobs. I would not expect a vice president to have 50 direct reports. They would not be able to spend the time they need with executives. Determine a reasonable number, but it should be at least 10.

I have seen organization charts where a vice president had one director working for him, and the director had one manager, and the manager had one analyst. I do not know why one analyst required 3 managers. It is obviously ridiculous. If the vice president needs an analyst, then the analyst should work for the vice president.

Reducing the number of people in a particular role is a much easier change than removing an entire layer of management. If desired, it can be done gradually by not replacing managers who retire or quit, instead moving their direct reports under a different manager.

Making Managers a Great Asset to the Company

M ost of this book has been more focused on the needs of the corporation. But what about the people who are in manager roles, many of whom have trained for nothing other than being a manager, and who are now concerned they will not have a job? Even if they still have a job, it may be a very different job than the one they trained for.

All managers, but especially line managers, should think of themselves as facilitators, coordinators, and coaches helping their teams work most efficiently by ensuring they have appropriate resources and removing roadblocks. Line managers in particular should use coaching practices such as asking questions, active listening, reflecting back, and silence to help team members figure out what to do themselves (instead of a manager telling them what to do).

A wise manager will strive to understand the work their teams do. Japanese companies such as Toyota have long had great success requiring their line managers to be people from the senior engineering ranks. As Google discovered, it is not required for a line manager to have the knowledge to mentor team members in their work, but it is very helpful if they can. A manager who is a great coach, really seeks to understand what the team does, provides resources for the team to be effective, but does not have experience in their field can be better for the team than one who can roll up their sleeves and do the work but does not help the team be their best.

Instead of a power hierarchy, middle manager roles can return to being directly related to the products and services of the company. As in the days of factories, middle managers can become deeply knowledgeable about the company products and services and the processes to provide them. Or a middle manager may become knowledgeable about the corporate capital assets and the processes to acquire and maintain them. Middle managers can observe those processes to discover inefficiencies and suggest ways to improve. Managers of all kinds can discover teams that are particularly good at their work, identify best practices, and share them with other teams. Middle managers can drive enterprise improvement efforts of all kinds. For this kind of work, getting a relevant certification such as Lean Six Sigma could be very beneficial.

Managers can be a great asset to a corporation when they focus on effectiveness and efficiency. A relatively flat organization chart speeds up communication throughout the company and saves money due to more people doing the work of the company and fewer people managing. The company saves more money over time with middle managers driving improvements in processes and line managers looking for ways to help their teams be more productive. The company also benefits by focusing on a few excellent managers rather than hiring a lot of managers to fill a hierarchy. For most companies, instead of thinking no managers think of a few great managers and help your existing managers become great.

Resources

This section is a list of links to websites I browsed to fill in some knowledge gaps and get more details. These web pages existed as of 27 January 2018.

Google

- http://www.businessinsider.com/google-on-habits-of-best-managers-2015-4
- http://www.businessinsider.com/larry-page-the-untold-story-2014-4
- https://images.forbes.com/media/2013/07/17/0717_oxygen-eight_742x807.jpg
- http://www.businessinsider.com/8-habits-of-highly-effective-google-managers-2011-3
- http://www.nytimes.com/2011/03/13/business/13hire.html?pagewanted=1&_r=1&ref=business&src=me
- https://hbr.org/2013/12/how-google-sold-its-engineers-on-management

Menlo Innovations

- Personal conversations with co-founder Thomas Meloche
- https://www.inc.com/winning-workplaces/magazine/201106/youll-never-work-alone.html
- https://www.forbes.com/sites/stevedenning/2016/08/02/the-joy-of-work-menlo-innovations/#3a9b8a935cf8
- https://www.inc.com/audacious-companies/leigh-buchanan/menlo-innovations.html

- http://menloinnovations.com/

The Morning Star Company

- Doug Kirkpatrick presentation at AgileCamp Silicon Valley 2017
- https://hbr.org/2011/12/first-lets-fire-all-the-managers
- https://www.inc.com/audacious-companies/leigh-buchanan/morning-star.html
- http://www.self-managementinstitute.org/assets/images/uploads/WhatIsSelfMgmt.pdf
- http://morningstarco.com/index.cgi?Page=About%20Us/Colleague%20Principles

U.S. Industrial Revolution

- http://www.ushistory.org/us/22a.asp
- http://www.history.com/topics/industrial-revolution
- https://www.thoughtco.com/overview-of-industrial-revolution-104721
- http://www.loc.gov/teachers/classroommaterials/primary-sourcesets/industrial-revolution/pdf/teacher_guide.pdf

Transcontinental Railway

- http://ushistoryscene.com/article/second-industrial-revolution/
- https://en.wikipedia.org/wiki/First_Transcontinental_Railroad
- http://www.generalcontractor.com/construction-resources/white-papers/historic-construction-projects/transcontinental-railroad.asp
- http://www.history.com/topics/inventions/transcontinental-railroad

History of Management

- https://medium.com/open-participatory-organized/a-brief-history-of-management-23361290a08b

- https://managementhelp.org/management/theories.htm
- https://hbr.org/2014/07/managements-three-eras-a-brief-history
- https://books.google.com/books?id=j3c8DwAAQ-BAJ&pg=PA57&lpg=PA57&dq=history+of+middle+manager&source=bl&ots=8CE-7WIy-c&sig=u637py-eYbe3T3U519H0FOTONRDA&hl=en&sa=X&ved=0a-hUKEwiB9K6h6aPYAhWK-VQKHfBEDPc4ChDoA-QhDMAY#v=onepage&q=history%20of%20middle%20manager&f=false
- https://en.wikipedia.org/wiki/Middle_management

About the Author

Geri Schneider Winters is a polymath with a wide range of interests. She loves bringing all that knowledge to bear when solving large, complex problems. Because of that, she is frequently found guiding business transformations at large companies.

In support of her business transformation work, Ms. Winters has studied and put into practice domains such as analysis, science of the brain, hypnosis, psychology, influence and advocacy, anthropology, philosophy, adult education, communication, marketing, interviewing, and a wide range of documentation techniques.

Ms. Winters explores her creative side with hobbies in healthy living, home brewing, cooking, photography, writing, book publishing, website creation, video production, singing, acting, and musical theater production. She has a deep love of the natural sciences and has been known to read physics "for fun", but admits to being "horrible" at tennis, basketball, and statistics.

Ms. Winters lives in a redwood forest on the Northern California coast with her husband and cats. She shares her property with deer, bunnies, skunks, foxes, many kinds of birds, and at least one bobcat. She is also within the territory of a mountain lion.

Visit Ms. Winters Amazon Author page to find her other titles: amazon.com/author/geriwinters

Other Books by this Author

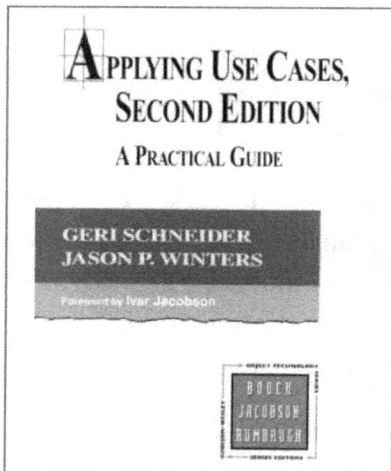

The original edition of Applying Use Cases was the first published book devoted to the topic of use cases - and an instant best seller. Schneider and Winters showed us not only how to write use cases, but what to do with them throughout a full incremental development lifecycle. The second edition was updated to UML 2.0 and expanded to show how to write use cases for business, and how to flow business use cases into software.

Applying Use Cases: A Practical Guide has been used in professional training in business analysis, Agile development, software architecture, and project management. It has also been the required text for project management courses at many universities.

This popular book has been continuously in print worldwide for over 15 years. It is available from Addision-Wesley Professional in US English, Polish, and Japanese editions.

Other Books by this Author

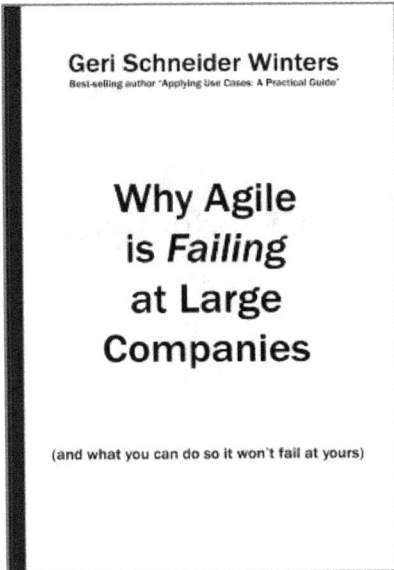

Geri Schneider Winters
Best-selling author "Applying Use Cases: A Practical Guide"

Why Agile is *Failing* at Large Companies

(and what you can do so it won't fail at yours)

This popular book on Agile debunks the many stories about how easy it is to bring Agile software development into large established companies. The truth is that changing your software development practices to be one flavor or another of Agile may be a bad thing for other parts of your company. Changing those other parts of your company so it all fits together again may be so expensive that the return on the investment is not worth it.

Before jumping on the Agile bandwagon, before starting down the path of tearing your company apart and rebuilding it, spend a little time investigating how big the change might be and if it will be worth it.

This 2015 book has been an Amazon Kindle best seller in Organizational Behavior, Problem Solving, and Management and Leadership.

The
Productivity Hacks Series

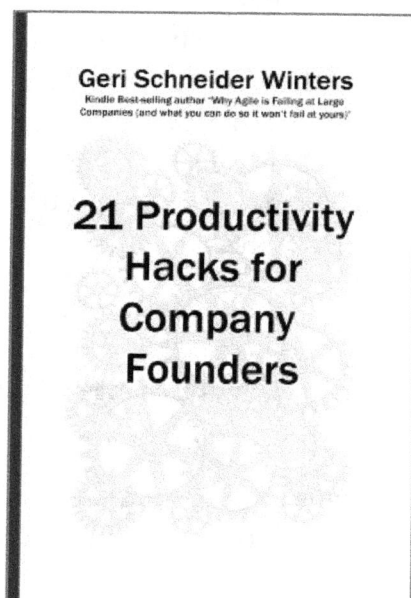

Geri Schneider Winters
Kindle Best-selling author "Why Agile is Failing at Large
Companies (and what you can do so it won't fail at yours)"

21 Productivity Hacks for Knowledge Workers

Geri Schneider Winters
Kindle Best-selling author "Why Agile is Failing at Large
Companies (and what you can do so it won't fail at yours)"

21 Productivity Hacks for Freelance Writers

Geri Schneider Winters
Kindle Best-selling author "Why Agile is Failing at Large
Companies (and what you can do so it won't fail at yours)"

21 Productivity Hacks for Company Founders